TADKA

BY SHAFU

BlueRose Publishers

© **Meenal Uppal 2020**

All rights reserved

All rights reserved by author. No part of this publication may be reproduced, stored in a retrieval system or transmitted in any form or by any means, electronic, mechanical, photocopying, recording or otherwise, without the prior permission of the author.

Although every precaution has been taken to verify the accuracy of the information contained herein, the author and publisher assume no responsibility for any errors or omissions. No liability is assumed for damages that may result from the use of information contained within.

First Published in October 2020

ISBN: 978-93-90396-64-1

BLUEROSE PUBLISHERS
www.bluerosepublishers.com
info@bluerosepublishers.com
+91 8882 898 898

Cover Design:
Anu Krishna

Typographic Design:
Namrata Saini

Distributed by: BlueRose, Amazon, Flipkart, Shopclues

Acknowledgement

This cookbook is dedicated to my mother, Lt. Smt. Usha Mahajan.

A mother is someone,
who can take the place of all others,
but, whose place no one else can take.

Thanks mom! We will keep you alive in our memories, carrying your legacy from one generation to the next.

Standard Weights & Measures

Abbreviations Used:

C - Cup
Tbsp - Tablespoon
tsp - Teaspoon
ml - Millilitre
g - Gram
kg - Kilogram
L - Litre

Liquid Measure Equivalents:

L – 1,000 ml
t / tsp – 5 ml
T / Tbsp – 15 ml
C – 240 ml

---

1 tsp = $\frac{1}{3}$ Tbsp = 5ml
3 tsp = 1 Tbsp = $\frac{1}{16}$ Cup = 15 ml
6 tsp = 2 Tbsp = $\frac{1}{8}$ Cup = 30 ml
12 tsp = 4 Tbsp = $\frac{1}{4}$ Cup = 60 ml
18 tsp = 6 Tbsp = $\frac{1}{3}$ Cup = 80 ml
24 tsp = 8 Tbsp = $\frac{1}{2}$ Cup = 125 ml
48 tsp = 16 Tbsp = 1 Cup = 250 ml
$\frac{2}{3}$ Cup = 160 ml
$\frac{3}{4}$ Cup = 180 ml
1$\frac{1}{2}$ Cup = 375 ml
2 Cup = 500 ml

Common Indian Names of Food Ingredients

Food Ingredients	Names in Hindi	Food Ingredients	Names in Hindi
Semolina	Suji	Bay Leaves	Tejpata
Whole-wheat flour	Atta	Whole red chilli	Sukhi lal mirch
Pigeon Peas	Arhar/tur dal/tuvar/toor	Black Onion Seeds	Kalonji
Cowpea	Lobia	Black Pepper	Kali Mirch
Green Gram	Moong	Black Salt	Kala Namak
Lentil	Masoor	Cardamom	Elaichi
Pink split dal	Masoor	Carom Seeds	Ajwain
Beetroot	Chukandar	Cinnamon	Dalchini
Colocasia	Arbi	Cloves	Long
Fenugreek Leaves	Methi	Coriander	Dhania
Raisin	Kishmish	Cumin Seeds	Jeera
Asafoetida	Hing	Nutmeg	Jaiphal
Fennel Seeds	Saunf	Pomegranate Seeds	Anardana
Garlic	Lehson	Poppy Seeds	Khuskhus
Ginger	Adrak	Red Chilli	Lal Mirch
Mace	Javithri	Saffron	Kesar
Mango Powder	Amchur	Tamarind	Imli
Mustard seeds	Rai/Sarson	Turmeric	Haldi

Contents

VEGETARIAN STARTERS

Paneer Tikka 2
Crispy Corn Chaat 5
Hara Bhara Kebab 8
Mumbai Vada Pav 10
Soya Chaap Tikka 14
Sabudana Tikki 18

NON-VEGETARIAN STARTERS

Amritsari Fish 22
Tangri Kebab 25
Chicken Pakora 28

VEGETARIAN DRY DISHES

Mixed Vegetable Sabzi 31
Dhaba Style Sukhe Aloo 34
Amla Ka Achar 37
Kurkuri Bhindi 39
Masala Arbi 43
Gobhi Manchurian 45

MAINS (VEGETARIAN)

Dal Makhani 50
Paneer Masala 53
Pindi Channa Masala 57
Shahi Paneer 62
Kadai Paneer 66
Dal Fry 70

MAINS (NON- VEGETARIAN)

Bhuna Gosht 74
Butter Chicken 77
Dum Chicken 81
Creamy Chicken 85

RICE & BREADS

Missi Roti 88
Aloo Masala Poori 91
Garlic Naan 95
Beetroot Poori 97
Spinach Poori 100
Vegetable Biryani 103
Channa Pulao 108
Tava Pulao 111
Chicken Biryani 114

Vegetarian Starters

PANEER TIKKA

Indian Restaurant-style Paneer Tikka at home with easy recipe

Preparation Time : 2 hours 15 minutes
Cooking Time : 20 minutes
Total Time : 2 hours 35 minutes
Servings : 3-4

Ingredients:

Cottage Cheese or Paneer - 200 g (Medium-size cubes)
Onion - 1 (diced into square-shaped sizes)
Green Capsicum - 1 (diced into square-shaped sizes)
Tomato (deseeded) - 1 (diced into square-shaped sizes)

For the Marinade:

*Hung Yoghurt - 1 Tbsp
Ginger/Garlic Paste – 1 tsp
Dried Fenugreek Leaves – 1 tsp
Roasted Gram Flour - 1¼ tsp
Cumin Powder – ½ tsp
Salt – 1 tsp
Turmeric Powder – ½ tsp
Red Chilli Powder - ½ tsp
Tandoori Masala – 1 tsp
Coriander Powder - ½ tsp
Garam Masala - ½ tsp
Mustard Oil – 1 Tbsp
Green Cardamom - 2-3 (crushed)
Green Chillies - 2 (finely chopped)

For Garnishing:

Butter – 1 tsp
Chat Masala – 1 tsp
Dried Fenugreek Leaves – ½ tsp
Lemon Juice - ½ tsp

*HUNG YOGHURT: Tie some yoghurt in a muslin cloth and leave it for at least 3-4 hrs, until all the water (whey) drains out to get a thicker consistency. That's when hung yoghurt is ready to use.

Instructions:

1. In a wide bowl, add hung yoghurt.
2. Whisk all the ingredients of the marinade like ginger/garlic paste, dried fenugreek leaves, roasted gram flour with dry spices like cumin powder, salt, tandoori masala, coriander powder, garam masala, mustard oil, turmeric powder, green cardamom, green chillies and red chilli powder along together.
3. Add the diced onion, capsicum, tomatoes and cottage cheese (paneer). Toss it gently.
4. Let the marinade rest for 2 hours.
5. Begin to thread the diced vegetables and cottage cheese (paneer) alternatively onto the skewer.
6. Heat some oil in a grill pan.
7. When the oil is hot enough, place the cottage cheese (paneer) and vegetable skewer on the pan and let it cook on medium flame.
8. Baste it with some butter and cook from all the sides.
9. When the cottage cheese (paneer) turns golden brown from both the sides, transfer the skewer to a serving plate.
10. Garnish it with crushed dried fenugreek leaves, chat masala and lemon juice.
11. Serve hot with chutney.

CRISPY CORN CHAAT

Quick Snack or Party Appetizer

Preparation Time : 15 minutes
Cooking Time : 15 minutes
Total Time : 30 minutes
Servings : 3

Ingredients:

For Boiling:
Sweet Corn Kernels - 1½ cup
Water - 2 cups

For Frying:
All-purpose Flour - 2 Tbsp
Corn flour - 2 Tbsp
Rice Flour – 2 Tbsp
Salt - to taste
Red Chilli Powder – ½ tsp
Water – 1 tsp

For Chaat:
Onion - 1 (small, finely chopped)
Capsicum – ¼ C (finely chopped)
Bell Peppers - ¼ C (finely chopped)
Red Bell Peppers - ¼ C (finely chopped)
Chat Masala - 1 tsp
Salt – ½ tsp
Coriander Leaves – 1 Tbsp
Lime juice – 1 tsp

Instructions:

1. Heat water in a large pan. Add the kernels and boil for 5-6 minutes or until they are softened.
2. Drain the water and spread the corn on a kitchen towel for an hour to remove the excess water.
3. Mix corn kernels, salt and chilli powder with corn flour, rice flour and all-purpose flour in a bowl.
4. Add some water if the mixture is too dry or some more corn flour and all-purpose flour if the mixture is too wet.
5. Heat oil in a frying pan.
6. Once the oil is hot enough for frying, take a few kernels and deep fry them in the oil.
7. Fry them on medium flame until they are crispy and golden brown and repeat the process with the rest of the kernels.
8. Transfer them onto an absorbent paper to remove the excess oil.
9. In a bowl, mix these fried kernels with chat masala, salt, onion, capsicum, bell peppers, coriander leaves and lime juice.
10. Toss them well and serve immediately.

HARA BHARA KEBAB

Tasty & healthy patties, full of greens and a plethora of spices

Preparation Time : 30 minutes
Cooking Time : 20 minutes
Total Time : 50 minutes
Servings : 5-6

Ingredients

Oil – 1 Tbsp.
Cumin Seeds – ½ tsp.
Ginger – ½ tsp. (finely chopped)
Garlic – ½ tsp. (finely chopped)
Green Chillies - 3 (finely chopped)
Fresh Green Peas – 1 ¼ cup
Spinach Leaves - 500 g (washed)
Fresh Coriander Leaves - 2 Tbsp. (chopped)
Salt - to taste
Garam Masala – ½ tsp.

Potatoes - 1 large (boiled, peeled and grated)
Bread Crumbs - 2 Tbsp. (optional)
Gram Flour or Besan – 1 Tbsp.
Oil - for deep frying

Instructions:

1. Dry roast gram flour till it turns aromatic. Set it aside.
2. Heat oil in a pan. Add cumin seeds and let the seeds splutter.
3. Add ginger and green chillies and sauté till raw aroma disappears.
4. Add peas and stir fry till tender. Add spinach and sauté until it wilts off completely.
5. Add salt and garam masala to it and sauté for a minute.
6. Put off the flame and let the mixture cool down completely.
7. Blend the spinach mixture along with the coriander leaves in a blender for a smooth paste. Note: Do not add any water.
8. Transfer this to a large mixing bowl. Mix the potatoes and gram flour to form a thick, non-sticky dough. (If sticky, add bread crumbs)
9. Dust your hands with the little breadcrumbs and roll the dough into round kebabs.
10. Heat oil in a frying pan for deep fry.
11. Deep fry kebabs in hot oil till golden brown and crisp or heat a nonstick pan with 2 Tbsp of oil and shallow fry till golden and crisp on both the sides.
12. Drain the excess oil from kebabs on an absorbent paper.
13. Sprinkle chat masala immediately after removing them from the oil.
14. Serve hot with coriander chutney.

MUMBAI VADA PAV

Deep-fried potato patties served inside a bread bun on Mumbai streets

Preparation Time : 30 minutes
Cooking Time : 20 minutes
Total Time : 40 minutes
Servings : 6-8

Ingredients

For Batter:
Besan - 1 cup
Salt - 1 tsp.
Red Chilli Powder – ¾ tsp.
Turmeric Powder – ½ tsp.
Water - 1 cup

For Vada:
Oil - 2 Tbsp
Mustard Seeds – 1 tsp
Asafoetida – ½ tsp
Curry Leaves – A Handful
Green Chilli - 1 finely chopped
Turmeric Powder – ½ tsp
Boiled Potatoes – 1 ½ cup
Salt – ¾ tsp

For Dry Garlic Chutney:
Oil - 2 Tbsp
Garlic Cloves - 12
Peanuts – ¼ cup
Sesame Seeds - 3 Tbsp
Red Chilli Powder – ½ Tbsp
Coriander Powder – ½ Tbsp
Salt – 1 tsp
Grated Coconut – ½ cup

Instructions

To Prepare Garlic Chutney:

1. Heat oil in a pan on a medium flame.
2. Add garlic and sauté for a few seconds.
3. Add peanuts, sesame seeds and dry roast them until seeds turns golden in colour.
4. Take off the flame and add chilli powder, coriander powder, salt and grated coconut.
5. Set the pan back on flame and cook again till the coconut is little roasted.
6. Transfer in a plate and let it cool.
7. Add the above mixture in a blender to make a coarse powder.

To Prepare Batter:

1. Whisk all the ingredients together for the batter including gram flour, salt, red chilli powder and turmeric powder except water.
2. Gradually, add enough amount of water to make a thick, lump-free batter. Keep it aside.

To Prepare Vada:

1. Heat oil in a pan and add asafoetida and mustard seeds.
2. Once, the mustard seeds begin to splutter, add green chillies and curry leaves and sauté for a few seconds.
3. Add turmeric powder and mix. Then, add in mashed potatoes, salt and mix well.
4. Let it cook for 2-3 minutes.
5. Take off from the heat and let the mixture cool down completely.

6. Divide the mixture and roll into balls then set them aside.
7. Heat oil for frying in a pan.
8. Dip each ball into the gram flour batter, with the help of a spoon to coat the mixture.
9. Deep-fry the coated balls in hot oil on a medium heat until golden brown.
10. Drain the excess oil on an absorbent paper and keep them aside.

Assembling:
1. Slice each pav into half, horizontally.
2. Spread some dry garlic chutney inside.
3. Place one hot vada on each slice.
4. Spread some garlic chutney again and cover with the other half.
5. Press down a little.
6. Serve with the deep fried green chillies.

SOYA CHAAP TIKKA

Snacks/Appetizers with a mesmerising taste

Preparation Time : 50 minutes
Cooking Time : 15 minutes
Total Time : 1 hour 5 minutes
Servings : 6-8

Ingredients:

Soya Chaap – ½ kg or 7-8 pcs
Yoghurt - 6 Tbsp
Kashmiri Red Chilli Powder - 3 tsp
Chat Masala – ½ tsp
Dried Fenugreek Leaves – 1 tsp (crushed)
Black Salt - 1 tsp
Cumin Powder – ½ tsp
Salt - to taste
Fresh Mint Leaves - 1 tsp
Black Pepper – ½ tsp
Melted Butter - 2 Tbsp
Turmeric Powder – ½ tsp
Cream - 2 Tbsp (optional)

For Assembling:

Onion - 1 (medium, sliced)
Coriander Leaves - 1 Tbsp (chopped)
Lemon Juice – 1 Tbsp
Green Chillies - 1 tsp (finely chopped)
Red Chilli Powder - 1 tsp
Chat Masala – ½ tsp
Garam Masala – ¼ tsp
Cream - 1 Tbsp
Melted Butter – 3 Tbsp (for brushing)

Instructions

To Prepare The Chaap:

1. Take some water in a vessel and add 1 Tbsp of salt in it. Keep this water for boiling on a medium low heat.
2. Add the Soya Chaaps in the boiling water. Allow it to boil for few minutes, till tender.
3. Drain and keep the soya chaaps aside. Let it cool.
4. Slit the chaaps vertically (lengthwise) into 2 pieces and then, horizontally into 2-3 pieces.
5. Keep them aside.

To Prepare The Marination:

1. In a separate bowl, whisk together yoghurt, Kashmiri red chilli powder, chat masala, dried fenugreek leaves, black salt, cumin powder, salt, garam masala, mint leaves, black pepper powder, turmeric powder and melted butter.
2. Now add cream (optional) and give it a gentle stir.
3. Add the soya chaap pieces into the marinade and mix it, until they are well-coated.
4. Let them rest for a minimum of 30 minutes.
5. Skewer the soya chaap pieces on a wooden skewer or steel skewers.
6. Bake them in an oven at 250°C for 10 minutes and baste (brush with butter) each of them after 5 minutes.
7. If you don't have an oven, heat a grill pan, add some butter to it and cook the soya chaap skewers on medium-high heat on each side for few minutes.

Make sure you cover them for few minutes while cooking which will ensure even cooking.

8. If you don't have either of them, insert the chaaps onto the steel skewers and roast them on the direct flame until the sides are browned.
9. Once it's done, brush the melted butter on each side of the chaap.
10. Again, char or brown the chaaps directly on the flame for at least a minute until the edges are blackened.
11. In a bowl, mix soya chaaps, coriander leaves, onion, green chillies, red chilli powder, chat masala, garam masala, cream and melted butter.
12. Toss it well.
13. Garnish with coriander leaves and serve.

SABUDANA TIKKI

A delicious, hot and crispy snack made of tapioca pearls

> *Preparation Time : 6 hours*
> *Cooking Time : 20 minutes*
> *Total Time : 6 hours 20 minutes*
> *Servings : 8-10*

Ingredients:

Sabudana or Sago – ½ cup

Water - 2 cups

Potato - 4 (medium, boiled and mashed)

Coriander Leaves - 2 Tbsp. (finely chopped)

Onion - 1 (medium, finely chopped)

Poppy Seeds or KhusKhus - 2 tsp (optional)

Ginger – 1 tsp. (finely chopped)

Green Chillies - 1 (finely chopped)

Chat Masala – ½ tsp.

Garam Masala – ½ tsp.

Red Chilli Powder – ½ tsp.

Mango Powder – ½ tsp.

Salt – ½ tsp.

Oil - for deep frying

Crushed Peanuts – 1 Tbsp.

Corn flour/bread crumbs – ¼ or ½ cup as required

Instructions:

1. Wash and clean the sabudana for atleast 3 times to clear the excessive starch.
2. Soak the sabudana in a sufficient amount of water for about 2-3 hours.
3. Drain the water and let it rest in the colander for about 5-6 hours or overnight.
4. In a bowl add the mashed potatoes and mix all the other ingredients like sabudana, coriander leaves, crushed peanuts, onion, poppy seeds, ginger, green chillies, chaat masala, garam masala, red chilli powder, mango powder, corn flour or breadcrumbs and salt.
5. Apply few drops of oil on your palm.
6. Roll the mixture into small balls.
7. Flatten each ball to shape it into round and flat tikkis.
8. Heat oil in a frying pan.
9. Deep or Shallow fry on a medium flame till they are crispy and golden. Do not overcrowd the frying pan.
10. Once cooked, place the tikkis on an absorbent paper to drain the excess oil.
11. Serve them hot.

Non-Vegetarian Starters

AMRITSARI FISH

Named after the city, made with fish fillet and a melange of Indian spices

Preparation Time : 15 minutes
Cooking Time : 15-20 minutes
Total Time : 30-40 minutes
Servings : 4-5

Ingredients:

Fish Fillet - 500 g (boneless and sliced)
Lemon – 1 juiced
Kashmiri Red Chilli Powder - 1 Tbsp.
Ginger, Garlic & green chilli paste - 1 Tbsp
Carom Seeds - ½ tsp.
Rice Flour - 1 tsp
Gram Flour - 1½ Tbsp.
Corn flour - 1 tsp
Turmeric - ¼ tsp
Salt - to taste
Asafoetida - a pinch
Water - to make the batter
Oil - for deep / shallow frying
Chat Masala - for sprinkling

Instructions:

1. In a bowl, add fish, sprinkle salt to taste and asafoetida.
2. Now add ginger paste, garlic paste, green chilli paste, lemon juice, Mix it gently. Let it set for 10 minutes at room temperature.
3. Once the fish has rested enough add rest of the ingredients, gram flour, corn flour, rice flour, carom seeds, red chilli powder, turmeric.
4. Gradually add enough water so that the masala coats the fish evenly from all the sides.
5. Now heat oil in a pan.
6. Deep / shallow fry the fish (2-3 pieces at a time) on medium flame till half done and cool.

7. Fry again in the hot oil till golden brown.
8. Place the fried fish in a serving bowl and squeeze some fresh lime juice on top of it and sprinkle with chat masala.
9. Serve fresh and hot.

TANGRI KEBAB

A very popular North-Indian starter recipe

Preparation Time : 10 minutes
Cooking Time : 20 minutes
Total Time : 30 minutes
Servings : 3-4

Ingredients:

Chicken Drumsticks - 4 pcs
Ginger Paste - 1 tsp
Garlic Paste - 1 tsp
Salt - $3/4$ tsp
Lime Juice - 1 Tbsp
Red chilli Powder - $3/4$ tsp
Hung Yoghurt - 2 Tbsp
Gram Flour - 2 tsp
Green Cardamom Powder – $1/8^{th}$ tsp
Mace Powder - a pinch
Dried Fenugreek Leaves – $1/4$ tsp (crushed)
Cream - 4 tsp

Instructions:

1. Take the chicken drumsticks and make a deep incision on each of the chicken legs on both sides.

2. For marination, whisk together salt, ginger-garlic paste, red chilli powder and lime juice. Add the chicken pieces and mix well.

3. Refrigerate the marinated chicken for 1 hour in the fridge.

4. In a bowl, whisk together the yoghurt, gram flour, pepper powder, cardamom powder, mace powder, dried fenugreek leaves, cumin powder and cream.

5. Add the marinated chicken to this and mix it well, ensuring that each chicken is well-coated with the mixture.

6. Refrigerate the marinated chicken for 6-8 hours, this time (or overnight for the best results).

7. If you have an oven, grill the marinated chicken in the preheated oven at 240°C for 20 minutes. Flip it once in between and baste it with butter.
8. Once the chicken is cooked, you can broil it till its slightly charred or brown by keeping it on the top shelf of the oven near the heat.
9. If you don't have an oven, transfer the entire marinated chicken onto a hot pan.
10. Cook it on medium heat. You will notice that the chicken will ooze out a lot of moisture. Just cook it till all the moisture dries out and the chicken is fully cooked.
11. Sprinkle some chat masala on the chicken pieces and squeeze lemon on it.
12. Serve hot with mint chutney.

CHICKEN PAKORA

Tiny, bite-sized boneless chicken fritters

Preparation Time : 20 minutes
Cooking Time : 15 minutes
Total Time : 35 minutes
Servings : 4-5

Ingredients:

Chicken - 500 g (boneless)
Ginger Paste – ¾ tsp
Garlic Paste – ¾ tsp
Garam Masala – 1 ½ tsp
Chilli Powder – 1 tsp
Pepper Powder – 1 tsp
Salt – 1 ½ tsp
Vinegar - 1 Tbsp
Oil – 1 Tbsp
Corn flour – ¾ cup
Gram Flour (Besan) - 2 Tbsp

Instructions:

1. Wash and pat dry the chicken and cut it into bite-sized pieces.
2. In a bowl, whisk together ginger paste, garlic paste, gram masala, chilli powder, pepper powder, salt, vinegar, oil, corn flour and gram flour. Add chicken pieces and toss well.
3. If required sprinkle 1 tsp of water if the mixture is too dry, ensuring all the pieces are well-coated with the marinade.
4. Refrigerate this mixture for 4 hours or overnight.
5. Heat oil in a pan for deep frying.
6. Deep-fry these chicken pieces in batches on a medium flame until the pakoras are nicely golden and crisp.
7. Drain the excess oil on an absorbent paper.
8. Serve with the mint chutney.

MIXED VEGETABLE SABZI

A North Indian delicacy cooked with vegetables and flavoured with fresh spices

Preparation Time : 15 minutes
Cooking Time : 40 minutes
Total Time : 55 minutes
Servings : 4-5

Ingredients:

(Vegetables can be added according to your choice)

Onions - 1 (big, finely chopped)

Cauliflower – ¼ cup (chopped)

French Beans – ¼ cup (chopped)

Carrot – ¼ cup (chopped)

Potatoes – ¼ cup (chopped)

Green Peas – ¼ cup

Coriander Leaves – ¼ cup

Cottage Cheese or Paneer – ¼ cup

Mushroom – ¼ cup

Cashew Nuts - 10-12 (chopped)

Clarified Butter (Ghee) - 4 Tbsp

Water - 4 cups

Coriander Leaves – ¼ cup (finely chopped)

Salt - to taste

Kashmiri Red Chilli Powder - 4 tsp

Turmeric Powder – 1 tsp

Coriander Powder – 1 tsp

Cumin Powder – 1 tsp

Garam Masala – ¼ - tsp

For Green Chili Paste:

Ginger – ½

Garlic - 3 cloves

Green Chillies – 1

Desiccated Coconut - 2 Tbsp (optional)

Instructions:

1. Blend the green chilli paste ingredients including the ginger, garlic, green chillies and Desiccated coconut in a grinder until it becomes a coarse paste.
2. Boil 4 cups of water. Add Ghee, chopped onions, cashew nuts, green chilli paste and dry spices like garam masala, Kashmiri red chilli powder, turmeric powder, coriander powder and cumin powder with finely chopped coriander leaves and ghee.
3. Add freshly chopped vegetables of your choice except paneer and add salt to taste and mix them well.
4. Let it boil and simmer half-covered so that the steam evaporates (keep gently stirring it in between) for 15-20 minutes or until the vegetables are cooked.
5. Add more hot water if vegetables are undercooked.
6. Remove the lid and add paneer cubes and mix.
7. Let it cook for a few more minutes on a medium-high flame to let the water evaporate completely and the vegetables are nicely coated with the masala.
8. Garnish with coriander leaves and serve it in a handi.

DHABA STYLE SUKHE ALOO

Tangy & Spicy potatoes

Preparation Time : 15 minutes
Cooking Time : 15 minutes
Total Time : 30 minutes
Servings : 3-4

Ingredients:

Boiled & Peeled Potatoes - 3 (medium, cut into bite-size pieces)
Bay Leaves - 2
Asafoetida – 1/8th tsp
Strained Yoghurt - ¼ cup
Oil or Clarified butter (Ghee) - 2 Tbsp
Water - 1-2 Tbsp
Coriander Leaves - for garnishing

For Spice Mix

Coriander Powder - 2 tsp
Mango Powder – ½ tsp
Pomegranate Seeds - 1 tsp
Cumin Seeds – ½ tsp
Red Chilli Powder – ½ tsp
Salt – ½ tsp
Black Salt – ¼ tsp
Garam Masala – ¼ tsp

Instructions:

1. Marinate the boiled potatoes along with the spices including coriander powder, mango powder, pomegranate powder, cumin powder, red chilli powder, salt, black salt and garam masala. Toss them well.
2. Let the potatoes rest for a minimum of 30 minutes.
3. Heat the clarified butter (ghee) in a pan and add asafoetida and bay leaves.
4. Add strained yoghurt and keep stirring for 2-3 minutes until the oil oozes out.
5. Add ¼ cup of water to this and stir.
6. Now, add the marinated potatoes. Mix them well and then, cover the lid. Let it cook for 2-3 minutes before removing it from the flame.
7. Let the potatoes rest for 5-10 minutes before serving.
8. Garnish with coriander leaves.

AMLA KA ACHAR

A healthy and delicious, Indian gooseberry pickle recipe which aids in digestion and is a good source of Vitamin-C

Preparation Time : 10 minutes
Cooking Time : 15 minutes
Total Time : 25 minutes
Servings : 5

Ingredients:

Amla (Gooseberry) - 250 g (deseeded and cut into bite-sized pieces)
Green Chillies - 3-4 (chopped 1-inch long)
Mustard Oil – 4 Tbsp
Asafoetida - A pinch
Cumin Seeds – ½ tsp
Carom Seeds – ½ tsp
Turmeric Powder – ½ tsp
Fennel Seeds powder - 1 tsp
Coriander Powder - 1 tsp
Salt - 1 tsp
Fenugreek Seeds – ¼ tsp

Instructions:

1. Heat oil in a pan and add the asafoetida, cumin seeds, carom seeds and fenugreek seeds. Let them splutter.

2. To this, add turmeric powder, coriander powder and fennel seeds powder.
3. Now, add the required amla and mix for 2-3 minutes. Add 1 tsp salt.
4. Cover the lid and let it cook on a low flame for 10 minutes or till the amla turns soft.
5. Amla fry is ready to be served.

Note: You can preserve amla fry in an airtight container for 10-12 days in a refrigerator.

KURKURI BHINDI

Spicy & crispy, deep-fried okras cooked with gram flour and spices

Preparation Time : 15 minutes
Cooking Time : 15 minutes
Total Time : 30 minutes
Servings : 3-4

Ingredients:

Okra (Bhindi) - 500 g

For Dry Spice Mix

Turmeric Powder – ¼ tsp
Red Chilli Powder - 1 tsp
Coriander Powder - 2 tsp
Cumin Powder – ½ tsp
Garam Masala – ½ tsp
Dry Mango Powder - 1 tsp
Rice Flour - 2 Tbsp
Gram Flour (Besan) - 4 Tbsp
Carom seeds – ¼ tsp
Lemon Juice – 1 tsp
Salt - to taste
Oil - for deep frying

Instructions:

1. Wash the okras thoroughly and pat dry. Remove their crowns and base tips.
2. Slice the bhindi vertically into 4 pieces. If you have long okras, then you will need to first slit them into 2 pieces horizontally. Remove the seeds.
3. Heat oil in a deep skillet on a medium heat.
4. Meanwhile, add the okras to a large mixing bowl, also add turmeric powder, red chilli powder, coriander powder, cumin powder, garam masala, and dry mango powder along with rice flour, gram flour and carom seeds. Do not add salt, else it will make the okra's soggy.

5. Add some lemon juice and mix thoroughly.
6. Fry the okras in batches by adding salt to taste and a tsp of water and mix it well.
7. Deep fry the okras in very hot oil for 2 minutes on high flame and then, on medium flame till they turn crispy.
8. Once done, remove and drain on the paper towel.
9. Repeat the same with the remaining okra batches.
10. Serve immediately.

MASALA ARBI

Known as Colocasia, a dry dish served usually with the main course on the sides

> **Preparation Time : 30 minutes**
> **Cooking Time : 30 minutes**
> **Total Time : 1 hour**
> **Servings : 2-3**

Ingredients:

Arbi/Colocasia - 500 g (Washed)
Salt - to taste
Coriander Powder – 1 ½ tsp
Red Chilli Powder – ¾ tsp
Turmeric Powder – ½ tsp
Dry Mango Powder – ¾ tsp
Rice Flour - 2 Tbsp
Mustard Seeds – 1 tsp
Cumin Seeds – ½ tsp
Asafoetida - a pinch
Oil - 2 Tbsp
Coriander Leaves - 1 Tbsp
Green Chillies - 2 (chopped)
Ginger – 1 (chopped)

Instructions:

1. Pressure cook the arbi in saltwater on medium flame for one whistle and let it depressurize on its own.
2. Let the arbi cool down completely and then peel.
3. Then, cut the arbi into ½ inch pieces. Grease your palms with some oil and lightly press and flatten the arbi.
4. In a bowl, add the arbi and dust the arbi with 2 Tbsp of rice flour and toss them well.
5. Heat 2 Tbsp oil in a pan and add cumin seeds, mustard seeds and carom seeds. Let them splutter.
6. Add the green chillies and chopped ginger. Sauté for a minute.
7. Add the arbi and let this cook for a minute on medium flame.
8. Add all the dry spices like coriander powder, red chilli powder, turmeric powder and dry mango powder to it.
9. Cover the lid and keep it for 2-3 minutes.
10. Now, add some garam masala and coriander leaves and again, cover it and let it cook for a minute.
11. Squeeze lime juice. Take it off the flame and serve.

GOBHI MANCHURIAN

Preparation Time : 15 minutes
Cooking Time : 20 minutes
Total Time : 35 minutes
Servings : 3-4

Ingredients:

For Blanching:
Cauliflower – 300 g (cut into small florets)
Salt – 1 tsp
Water – 3 Cups

For The Marinade:
Ginger Garlic Paste - 1 Tbsp
Salt – ½ tsp
Black Pepper – ½ tsp
Cornstarch – ¼ cup

For The Batter:
All-purpose Flour – ½ Cup
Cornstarch – ¼ Cup
Salt - 2 Tbsp
Oil - For Deep frying

For the Sauce Mix:
Water – ¼ Cup
Soya Sauce – 2 Tbsp
Vinegar – 1 ½ tsp
Chilli Garlic Paste – 1 Tbsp
Tomato Sauce – 1 Tbsp
Hoisin Sauce – 1 tsp (optional)
Cornstarch – 1 Tbsp

For the manchurian
Oil - 2 Tbsp

Onions - 3 Tbsp (finely chopped)

Garlic - 5-6 pods (finely chopped)

Ginger – 1 ½ tsp (finely chopped)

Capsicum - 1 (small, finely chopped)

Instructions:

Cauliflower Marination:

1. Wash and clean the cauliflower properly.
2. Boil 3 cups of water with salt in a pan.
3. Add the cauliflower. Cover and let it cook for 5-7 minutes till the cauliflower is soft.
4. Strain the cauliflower and rinse it with cold water. Keep it aside.
5. In a bowl, combine cauliflower with ginger garlic paste. Toss it well.
6. Add salt, black pepper and cornstarch. Give it a nice mix and let the marinade rest in the refrigerator for 15-20 minutes.

To Prepare The Batter:

1. In a separate bowl, mix all-purpose flour, cornstarch, oil and salt.
2. Gradually, add water and beat it nicely to make a thick coating consistency.
3. Heat oil for deep frying in a wok till medium hot.
4. Dip the marinated florets in the batter and deep fry them on medium-high heat till half done. (Do not overcrowd the kadai). Place the fried florets on the absorbent paper to drain the excess oil.

5. Re-fry the fried cauliflower again on a high heat till they turn golden in colour and repeat the process.

To prepare the sauce:

Mix water, soya sauce, vinegar, chilli garlic paste, tomato ketchup, hoisin sauce (optional) and corn flour. Stir and keep it aside.

For serving:
1. Heat 2 Tbsp of oil in a wok.
2. Add chopped onions, ginger, garlic and capsicum. Sauté for a minute.
3. Add the sauce mix, salt, and black pepper to taste.
4. Give it a boil, till the sauce thickens. Put off the flame. Let it cool down for a few seconds till the smoke completely settles down.
5. Mix the fried cauliflowers in this sauce, ensuring that the spiced sauce coats the cauliflower florets perfectly.
6. Garnish with spring onions and serve hot.

Mains (Vegetarian)

DAL MAKHANI

Rich and flavourful black lentils cooked with butter and cream

Preparation Time : 20 minutes
Cooking Time : 2 hours
Total Time : 2 hours 20 minutes
Servings : 4-5

Ingredients:

Whole Urad Dal – ¾ Cup
Rajma – ¼ Cup
Channa Dal - 2 Tbsp
Clarified Butter (Ghee) - 1 tsp
Ginger-Garlic Paste - 1 Tbsp
Salt - to taste
Asafoetida - a pinch
Clarified Butter (Ghee) - 1 tsp
Butter - 2 Tbsp (optional)
Onion - 1 medium (finely chopped)
Tomato Puree - 3 (medium-sized)
Kashmiri Red Chilli Powder – 1 tsp
Nutmeg Powder - a pinch
Yoghurt – 2 Tbsp
Milk – ½ Cup
Cream – ¼ Cup
Dried Fenugreek Leaves – ¼ tsp

Instructions:

1. Mix the urad dal, Rajmah and Channa dal together and wash properly. Soak it in water overnight.

2. Drain the water and pressure cook along with 3 cups of water, clarified butter (ghee), and asafoetida.

3. Pressurecook it on a high flame for 1 whistle and for 6-7 whistles on low flame till it's perfectly cooked and softened.

4. Heat Ghee in a pan.

5. Add onions and sauté till translucent. Then, add the ginger-garlic paste and cook until the raw aroma disappears.
6. Add green chillies and sauté till the onion turns brown (add 1 Tbsp of water if required).
7. Add red chilli powder and nutmeg powder. Mix
8. Add tomato puree and salt to taste and sauté till oil separates.
9. Then, add yoghurt and keep stirring on medium-low flame for about 10 minutes, till the oil oozes out.
10. Now, add the dal to this mixture and stir it well. Add if more salt is required.
11. Cook for 10-15 minutes and add some milk and give it a stir.
12. Simmer the dal (uncovered) on a low flame, keep stirring in between so that the dal doesn't stick to the bottom of the pan. You can add some more hot water if the gravy looks too thick or dry.
13. Add 2 Tbsp of butter. Let it cook on a low flame for a minimum of half an hour. The longer you let the dal cook on simmer, the better it tastes.
14. When the gravy is thick enough, add ¼ cup of cream. (Do not boil)
15. Now, add dried crushed fenugreek leaves. Mix and serve immediately.

Note: Dal makhani is neither too thick nor too runny. It has a medium consistency.

PANEER MASALA

Dhaba-style paneer or cottage cheese recipe

Preparation Time : 15 minutes
Cooking Time : 20 minutes
Total Time : 35 minutes
Servings : 3-4

Ingredients:

For The Paneer Marinade:

Cottage Cheese/Paneer – 300 g (cut into cubes)
Kashmiri Red Chilli Powder - 1 tsp
Garam Masala – ½ tsp
Turmeric Powder – ¼ tsp
Water - 2 Tbsp
Salt – 1 tsp
Clarified butter (ghee) -1 Tbsp

For The Gravy:

Onion - 3 (medium, finely chopped)
Tomato - 3 (medium, grated)
Ginger – 1 (finely chopped)
Garlic - 5 (finely chopped)
Green Chillies - 2 (sliced lengthwise)
Yoghurt – ½ Cup (whisked & sieved)
Mustard Oil - 2 Tbsp
Water - 1 cup
Clarified butter(ghee) - 1 tsp
Oil – 1 Tbsp
Dried fenugreek leaves (kasuri Methi)- ½ tsp

For Dry Spice Mix:

Turmeric Powder – ½ Tsp

Salt - to taste

Dried crushed Fenugreek Seeds – 1 ½ Tbsp

Garam Masala – ½ -1 tsp

Coriander Powder - 2 tsp

Roasted Cumin Powder – 1 tsp

Red Chilli Powder – 1 tsp

Kashmiri Red Chilli Powder – 1 tsp

Gram Flour (Besan) - 2 tsp

For Whole Spice Mix:

Black Peppercorns – 4-5

Cloves – 4-5

Green Cardamom - 2

Bay Leaf - 2

Black Cardamom - 1

Cinnamon - 1

Dried Red Chillies - 2

Cumin Seeds – ½ tsp

Instructions:

1. To marinate the paneer : In a bowl, mix the cottage cheese (paneer) with salt, Kashmiri red chilli powder, garam masala and turmeric powder.
2. Toss it well so that the cottage cheese (paneer) is well-coated with the masala.
3. Now, add 2 Tbsp of water and toss it gently. Let it rest for 30 minutes.

4. After 30 minutes shallow fry the paneer cubes in 1 Tbsp of ghee for a minute on high flame and keep it aside

5. Heat a pan and dry roast the whole spices like black peppercorns, cloves, green cardamom, bay leaf, black cardamom, cinnamon, dried red chillies and cumin seeds on a medium flame till it becomes fragrant. Keep it aside.

6. Heat another pan, add ghee and onions to this and fry them on a medium flame till they turn brown.

7. Then, add chopped ginger and garlic to it and fry till the raw aroma disappears and add 1 tsp of water to avoid onions sticking to the pan and fry till the onions turns dark brown.

8. In a bowl, add oil and mix all the dry spices like turmeric powder, coriander powder, roasted cumin, red chilli powder, Kashmiri red chilli powder, and gram flour.

9. Add this oil mixed dry spices to the onions and sauté for 15-20 seconds.

10. Now, add tomatoes, green chilies, roasted whole spices and salt. Cover the lid and cook till the oil oozes out.

11. Add yoghurt and cook on a low flame while stirring continuously for around 5-10 minutes until the yoghurt is fully infused in the gravy and oozes out oil.

12. Add garam masala and crushed fenugreek leaves and mix it well.

13. Add 1-2 cups of water to adjust the desired consistency. Give it a boil.

14. Add the cooked cottage cheese (paneer) cubes to this and toss it well.

15. Cover the lid and let it cook for about 5-7 minutes on a low flame till the oil starts floating on the surface.

16. Garnish with coriander leaves.

17. Serve hot.

PINDI CHANNA MASALA

A classic Punjabi delicacy made with Kabuli Channa

> *Preparation Time : 10 minutes*
> *Cooking Time : 20 minutes*
> *Total Time : 30 minutes*
> *Servings : 4-5*

Ingredients:

Kabuli Channa or Chickpeas - 1 cup (washed & soaked overnight)
Bay Leaf - 2
Cloves - 3-4
Teabags - 1
Salt - 2 tsp
Oil - 2 Tbsp
Black Cardamom - 2
Green Cardamom - 2-3
Dried Gooseberry/Amla - 2-3
Cinnamon Sticks - 2-3
Baking Soda – 1/8 tsp
Water – 2 ½ - 3 cups
Tomato - 2 (pureed)
Ginger-Garlic Paste – 1 ½ tsp
Onion - 1 (medium-size, grated)

For Dry Spice Mix:

Channa Masala - 2 Tbsp (Recipe mentioned below)
Red Chilli Powder - 1 tsp
Turmeric Powder – ½ tsp
Coriander Powder - 1 tsp
Pomegranate Seeds Powder - 1 tsp

For Tempering:

Clarified Butter (Ghee)– 3 Tbsp
Ginger - 1 inch cut into Julienne

Green Chillies - 3 (slits, lengthwise)
Asafoetida – ¼ tsp
Dried Fenugreek Leaves - 1 tsp
Red chilli powder - 1 tsp
Chopped Coriander Leaves - for garnishing

Instructions:

1. Pressure cook the chickpeas along with water, baking soda, dried gooseberry, salt, teabags and whole spices like bay leaf, cinnamon sticks, black cardamom, cloves and green cardamom till 4-5 whistles. Let it depressurize on its own.
2. Strain the boiled chickpeas and keep the chickpeas and water aside.
3. Discard the teabags and the whole spices.
4. Heat 2 Tbsp of oil in a pan. Add the onion paste to it.
5. Sauté till the onions turn golden brown. Add little water if the onion paste starts sticking to the bottom of the pan.
6. Now, add in the ginger-garlic paste. Sauté till the raw aroma disappears.
7. Add tomato puree and salt. Cook it on a medium-high flame till the oil oozes out.
8. Then, add all the dry spices including Channa masala, coriander powder, pomegranate seeds powder, red chilli powder and turmeric.
9. Sauté for a few seconds and add boiled Channa to it. Mix well.
10. Now, add the remaining Channa water to this.
11. Cover the lid and let it cook on a medium-low flame for 2-3 minutes.
12. Then, mash the Channa little with the help of a spatula.

13. Cover the lid and let it cook for another 2-3 minutes till the oil oozes out and floats on the surface. If you wish to have more gravy, you can add more hot water.
14. Add the crushed dried fenugreek leaves and mix.

For Tempering:
1. Heat the ghee in a pan. Add asafoetida.
2. Add the slits of green chillies.
3. Then, put of the flame and add red chilli powder.
4. Pour it over the Channa and garnish it with coriander leaves and ginger julienne.
5. Serve hot.

For Channa Masala:

Ingredients:

Whole Cumin Seeds - 4 tsp
Whole Coriander Seeds - 2 tsp
Black Cardamoms - 2
Cloves - 10
Black Whole Pepper - 15
Cinnamon Sticks - 3
Bay Leaf - 4
Dried Fenugreek Leaves - 2 Tbsp

Carom Seeds – 1 tsp
Whole Red Chillies - 4
Pomegranate Seeds - 1 tsp
Black Salt - 2 Tbsp

Instructions:

1. First, dry roast all the ingredients together.
2. Then, grind it in a dry spice mixer and add black salt at the end.

SHAHI PANEER

A flavourful, Punjabi version of paneer with an aromatic, rich and creamy gravy

Preparation Time : 5 minutes
Cooking Time : 30 minutes
Total Time : 35 minutes
Servings : 5

Ingredients:

Paneer/Cottage Cheese - 250 g (cut into cubes)

For The Gravy:

Onion – 1 Cup (boiled & pureed)
Tomatoes – 4-5 (medium size, chopped)
Ginger-Garlic paste – 1 tsp
Black Cardamom/MotiElaichi – 2
Green Chillies - 2 (split into halves)
Cashew Nuts - 6-8 (for the paste)
Strained yoghurt – ¼ Cup
Cream - 1 Cup
Garam Masala – ½ tsp
Kashmiri Red Chilli Powder - 1 tsp
Salt - to taste
Tomato Ketchup - 2-3 tsp (optional)
Warm Milk - 1 Cup
Ghee - 3 Tbsp
Dried fenugreek leaves– 1 tsp (Crushed)
Coriander Leaves - for garnishing

Instructions

For The Cashew Nut Paste:

1. Soak the cashew nuts in hot water for about 30 minutes. Drain the water and grind the cashew nuts into a fine powder.
2. Gradually, add water to the granulated cashews and grind it to have a fine paste.
3. If the mixture is grainy in texture, add some more water and keep grinding the cashews until you get the desired consistency – smooth and creamy.

For The Paneer Gravy:

1. Heat 2 Tbsp of ghee in a pan. Add black cardamom, green chillies, ginger-garlic paste and onion to it. Cook until the onion turns light brown.
2. Add in the chopped tomatoes. Cover and cook it on a low flame till the tomatoes turn pulpy.
3. Put off the flame and let it cool down.
4. Blend the cooked tomatoes into a smooth paste. Pass through a fine sieve.
5. Now, heat 1 Tbsp of ghee in a pan. Add kashmiri red chilli powder. Immediately add the strained puree and Salt. Sauté for 8-10 minutes till the colour of the puree changes.
6. To this, add the cashew nut paste. Cover the lid and let it cook for 3-4 minutes.
7. Add the beaten curd. Keep stirring gradually.
8. Cover and cook it again, till all the oil oozes out.
9. Then, add milk and 1 cup of water (depending on the consistency you wish to achieve). Give it 5-6 boils.

10. Add garam masala, elaichi powder and ketchup (optional) to this. Boil it for 5-7 minutes. You can also add 1 tsp of corn flour paste (corn flour mixed with water) if the consistency of the gravy is too thin.
11. Now, add the paneer cubes and crushed fenugreek leaves at the time of serving. Cover it for 2 minutes.
12. Gradually, add some cream to the gravy. (Do not boil)
13. Garnish it with swirls of beaten cream and a bunch of coriander leaves.
14. Serve hot.

KADAI PANEER

A uniquely flavoured, semi-dry cottage cheese and bell pepper dish cooked with freshly ground spices

Preparation Time : 15 minutes
Cooking Time : 25 minutes
Total Time : 40 minutes
Servings : 4-5

Ingredients:

Paneer - 400 g (cut into cubes)
Oil - 2 Tbsp
Onion - 4 (medium, roughly chopped)
Tomato - 6 (medium, roughly chopped)
Onion - 1 (medium, cut into cubes)
Green Capsicum - 1 (cut into cubes)
Dried Fenugreek leaves - 1 Tbsp
*Kadai Masala - 1- 2 tsp
Water - 1/2 - 1 Cup
Ginger-Garlic Paste – 1 Tbsp
Green chillies - 2 (slit lengthwise)
Cloves - 4-5
Bay Leaf - 2
Black Cardamom - 1
Green Cardamom - 2

Black Peppercorns - 4-5
Cinnamon Stick - 1
Dried Red Chillies - 2
Salt – 1 ½ tsp
Cumin Powder – ½ tsp
Coriander Powder - 3 tsp
Turmeric Powder – ½ tsp
Kashmiri Red Chilli - 1 tsp
Red Chilli Powder – ½ tsp (optional)

For Kadai Masala
Dried Red Chillies - 1
Fennel Seeds – ½ tsp
Cumin Seeds - 1 tsp
Coriander Seeds - 1 Tbsp
Black Peppercorns – ½ tsp

Instructions:

1. To make the kadai masala, dry roast red chilli, fennel seeds, cumin seeds, coriander seeds, and peppercorns till the mixture is fragrant. Let it cool down and then, grind it into a smooth powder. Store it in an airtight container.
2. Heat oil in a pan. Add the chopped onions and sauté till it turns brown.
3. Then, add in the chopped tomatoes and salt. Cover the lid and let it cook, till the tomatoes become mushy. Put off the flame and let the mixture cool down.
4. Once it's cooled down, grind it to make thick paste with the grounded kadai masala in a grinder by adding some water. Keep it aside.
5. Take another pan and dry roast the garam masala, black pepper, cloves, green cardamom, bay leaf, black cardamom, and cinnamon sticks (do not burn the spices) till it's fragrant.
6. Add 2 Tbsp of ghee/oil and add the ginger-garlic paste to it and sauté till the raw aroma disappears.
7. Add the green chillies and sauté for a few seconds. Add the onion cubes and let it cook for 2-3 minutes. Then, add the capsicum cubes and sauté till the onion turns translucent.
8. To this, add the onion tomato paste and all the dry spices like coriander powder, cumin powder, Kashmiri red chilli powder, red chilli powder, turmeric and salt to taste, (as have already added salt in the onion and tomato paste) mix well.
9. Add $1/2$ -1 cup water and give it a stir. Cover the lid and cook the vegetables till they're soft.
10. Add some cream (optional) on a low flame and dried fenugreek leaves and stir.

11. Now add the cottage cheese (paneer) cubes to this gravy. Toss it. Cover the lid and let it cook for 2-3 minutes.
12. Once it's done, add a few coriander leaves and give it a nice mix.
13. Garnish it with some butter.
14. Serve hot.

DAL FRY

A Dhaba-style lentil recipe, famous in all Indian restaurants

Preparation Time : 15 minutes
Cooking Time : 20 minutes
Total Time : 35 minutes
Servings : 4-5

Ingredients:

Pigeon Peas (Arhar Dal) – ½ Cup (washed & soaked for 20 minutes)
Masoor Dal (Pink Split Dal) – ½ Cup (washed & soaked for 20 minutes)
Green Chillies - 2 (finely chopped)
Onions - 2 (medium size, finely chopped)
Tomatoes - 2 (medium size, finely chopped)
Ginger - garlic paste – 1 tsp
Turmeric Powder – 1 tsp
Salt - to taste
Garam Masala - a pinch
Asafoetida - a pinch
Water – 2 ½ Cups
Fenugreek Leaves - 1 tsp (roasted and crushed)
Fresh Cream - 2 Tbsp (optional)

For Tempering:

Clarified Butter (Ghee) - 2 Tbsp
Cumin Seeds - 1 tsp
Garlic - 5-6 cloves (finely chopped)
Whole Dry Red Chillies - 2-3
Asafoetida - a pinch
Red Chilli Powder – ½ tsp
Curry Leaves - 8-10

For Garnishing:

Garam Masala – ¼ tsp
Coriander Leaves – 1 Tbsp

Instructions:

1. In a pressure cooker, add the arhar and masoor dal along with chopped onions, green chillies, tomatoes, ginger-garlic paste, asafoetida, salt, turmeric powder and water.
2. Pressure cook the dal on a high flame for 4 whistles and then, simmer for about 5 minutes till they become soft and creamy.
3. Let the pressure depressurize on its own.
4. Now, whisk the dal with a ladle.
5. Then, add the dried fenugreek leaves , chopped coriander leaves and cream (optional). Keep it aside. Add if more salt is required before adding the tempering.

For Tempering:

1. Heat 2 Tbsp of clarified butter (ghee) in a pan. Add cumin seeds and let them splutter.
2. Add the whole dry red chillies and garlic. Let the garlic turn brown and then, add some curry leaves.
3. To this, add the red chilli powder and turn off the gas immediately.
4. Pour the tempering into the dal.
5. Garnish it with garam masala and coriander leaves.
6. Serve hot.

Mains (Non-Vegetarian)

BHUNA GOSHT

Dhaba-style, roasted chicken gravy

Preparation Time : 30 minutes
Cooking Time : 40 minutes
Total Time : 1 hour 10 minutes
Servings : 3-4

Ingredients:

For The First Marination:

Chicken - 500 g
Ginger Paste - 1 tsp
Garlic Paste - 1 tsp
Red Chilli Powder - 1 tsp
Cumin Powder – ½ tsp
Lemon – 1 Juiced
Salt – 1 tsp

For The Gravy:

Cumin Seeds – ½ tsp
Whole Red Chillis - 2
Cloves - 3
Black Peppercorns - 5-6
Green Chillies – 3-4
Kashmiri Red Chilli Powder - 2 tsp
Red Chilli Powder - 1 tsp (optional for extra spice)
Coriander Powder - 3 tsp
Gram Flour - 2 tsp
Fennel Seeds - 1 tsp
Mustard Oil - 2 Tbsp
Onion - 3 (finely chopped)
Tomatoes - 6 (grated)
Butter - a dollop
Dried Fenugreek Leaves - 1 tsp
Black Onion Seeds (Kalonji) – ¼ tsp
Coriander Leaves – a handful (for garnishing)

Instructions:

1. Place the chicken pieces in a bowl, add ginger - garlic paste, salt, red chilly powder, cumin powder and lemon juice, mix well. Let the chicken marinate settle for half an hour in a refrigerator.

2. Heat a pan and dry roast all the whole spices cumin seeds, cloves, black peppercorns, green cardamom and whole red chillies together, till the mixture becomes fragrant. Remove and keep it aside.

3. In a pressure cooker, heat mustard oil. Now, add onions and fry them on a medium heat for 10 minutes till they turn golden brown.

4. Now, add the ginger-garlic paste, turmeric powder, kashmiri red chilli powder, red chilli powder, coriander powder, gram flour and fennel seeds and 1 Tbsp of water.

5. Fry again till the onions turn dark brown.

6. Now, add the grated tomatoes, green chillies and salt and all the roasted whole spices.

7. Sauté for 10-15 minutes until the oil oozes out and the mixture turns almost dry.

8. Add the marinated chicken to this mixture and let it roast on a high heat for a minute until the chicken changes its colour.

9. Add 1 ½ cups of water. Pressure cook the chicken for 1 whistle on a medium flame. Put off the flame.

10. Let it depressurize on its own.

11. Add the crushed fenugreek leaves, garam masala and black onion seeds. (If you like a thick gravy, then cook it uncovered on a high flame till you get the desired consistency)

12. Now, garnish with a dollop of butter and coriander leaves and serve.

Note : How to use Mustard oil for cooking - heat it to smoking point and then cool it to required temperature before using it for cooking preparations.

BUTTER CHICKEN

A Homemade chicken dish with a rich, tomato-based creamy sauce

Preparation Time : 5 minutes
Cooking Time : 30 minutes
Total Time : 35 minutes
Servings : 5-6

Ingredients:

Chicken Breast - 500 g (boneless, cut into bite-size pieces)

For The Marination:
Ginger- Garlic paste Paste – 1 tsp
Red Chilli Powder – 1 tsp
Cumin Powder – ½ tsp
Coriander Powder – 1 tsp
Garam Masala Powder – ¼ tsp
Dried fenugreek leaves - ½ tsp (crushed)
Salt - to taste
Yoghurt - 2 Tbsp
Cream - 2 Tbsp
Oil - 1 Tbsp

For Preparing The Chicken:
Ghee – 1 Tbsp
Cinnamon - 1
Bay Leaf - 1
Green Cardamom - 12
Onions - 2 (roughly chopped)
Tomatoes - 6 (roughly chopped)
Ginger- Garlic paste - 2 tsp
Kashmiri Red chilli powder - ½ tsp
Sugar / Honey - ½ tsp
Cashew Nuts – ½ Cup
Butter - 50 g

Cream – ¼th Cup

Dried Fenugreek Leaves – ½ tsp

Water - 2 cups

Instructions

For The Chicken:

1. In a bowl, whisk together all the ingredients for the marination, ginger-garlic paste, red chilli powder, cumin powder, coriander powder and garam masala, dried fenugreek leaves, cream with yoghurt, salt and oil.
2. Add the chicken pieces and mix them well, ensuring that all the pieces are well-coated with the marinade. Refrigerate them for 1 hour.
3. Roast the marinated chicken pieces in a pan or grill or in the oven, till it is ¾th cooked.
4. Once that's done, keep it aside in a bowl.

For The Gravy:

1. In a bowl, mix together onions, tomatoes, cashew nuts and all the whole spices like cardamom, bay leaf, and cinnamon along with 2 cups of water.
2. Cover the lid. Let it simmer for 20 minutes or until the vegetables turns soft.
3. Let the mixture cool down and discard the whole spices.
4. Then, churn the mixture into a fine puree. Strain and keep it aside.
5. Now, heat some ghee in a deep pan and add the ginger-garlic paste to it. Sauté and fry, till the raw aroma disappears.

6. Add the Kashmiri red chilli powder and immediately add strained onion and tomato puree and let it cook for 6-7 minutes or till the colour of the gravy changes.

7. Add the semi cooked chicken pieces.

8. Then, add salt to taste, sugar and sprinkle the crushed dried fenugreek leaves.

9. Let it cook for another 5 -7 minutes.

10. Add the butter to this gravy. Cover the lid and cook the gravy on low flame till the chicken is completely cooked, until you get the desired consistency.

11. Add cream on low flame (Do not boil). Then, put off the flame.

12. Garnish it with some more cream and dried fenugreek leaves on top and serve.

DUM CHICKEN

A flavourful and aromatic, slow-cooked chicken curry

Preparation Time : *10 minutes*
Cooking Time : *30 minutes*
Total Time : *40 minutes*
Servings : 3-4

Ingredients:

Chicken – 750 g (with bones)
Hung Yoghurt - 150 g
Brown Fried Onions* - 3 (medium-sized, crushed)
Ginger – 1 tsp
Garlic – 1 tsp
Coriander Leaves - 1 Cup (finely chopped)
Salt - to taste
Turmeric Powder – ½ tsp
Red Chilli Powder - 2 tsp
Garam Masala - 2 tsp
Black Pepper Powder – ½ tsp
Cumin Powder – ½ tsp
Green Cardamom Powder – 1/8 tsp
Coriander Powder – ½ tsp
Saffron Milk – a pinch of saffron mixed with ¼ Cup of warm milk
Lemon - 1 Juiced
Oil - 2 Tbsp
Clarified Butter (Ghee) – 1 tsp

For Cashew Nut Paste:

Cashew Nuts - 8
Almonds - 8
Grated Coconut - 2 Tbsp
Green chillies - 1 finely chopped

Instructions

* To Prepare The Brown Fried Onions:

1. Heat the oil for deep frying in a pan.
2. Add the finely sliced onions and deep fry till they turn golden brown.
3. Strain and keep it on an absorbent paper to remove the excess oil.
4. They are now ready to use.

To Prepare The Chicken:

1. Take the chicken and make a deep incision on each chicken piece on both sides.
2. Squeeze lemon juice on each of them and keep them aside for 10 minutes.
3. Heat a pan and dry roast (without oil) a few almonds, cashew nuts and grated coconut for 2-3 minutes.
4. Let it cool down and then add chopped green chillies and grind it into a fine paste along with some water to make a thick paste.
5. Keep the paste aside.

To Marinate The Chicken:

1. Take a mixing bowl and whisk together the yoghurt, ginger-garlic paste, coriander powder, turmeric powder, red chilli powder, garam masala, black pepper powder, cumin powder, cardamom powder along with saffron milk, cashew nut paste, lemon juice, crushed fried onions, salt and coriander leaves.
2. Add the chicken pieces to it and mix them well, ensuring that all the chicken pieces are well-coated with the marinade.
3. Refrigerate the marinated chicken for 2 or 2 ½ hours.

For the Gravy :

1. Heat 1 Tbsp oil in a heavy bottom pan and add the marinated chicken to it. Let it cook on a medium flame until it starts boiling.
2. Now, add 1 tsp of Ghee . Cover the lid and cook it on dum (slow flame), stirring once after every 10 minutes. Make sure that there is enough water to cook the chicken.
3. Let the chicken simmer for 30 minutes or till it's perfectly cooked.
4. Serve hot.

CREAMY CHICKEN

A classic, creamy and saucy chicken dish that you won't be able to get enough of

Preparation Time : 5 minutes
Cooking Time : 10 minutes
Total Time : 15 minutes
Servings : 3-4

Ingredients:

Chicken - 500 g
Oil - 1 Tbsp
Butter - 1 Tbsp
Garlic Paste – 1 tsp
Ginger Paste – 1 tsp
Dried Fenugreek Leaves - 2 Tbsp
Thick Yoghurt – ¾ Cup (strained)
Salt – ¼ tsp
Pepper – ¼ tsp
Green Chillies – 1 or 2 (split lengthwise)
Coriander Leaves - 2 Tbsp
Fresh Cream - 4 Tbsp
Butter – a dollop (for garnishing)

Instructions:

1. Heat 1 Tbsp of oil in a pressure cooker.
2. Add the ginger-garlic paste and sauté till the raw aroma disappears.
3. To this, add all the chicken pieces. Sauté for 1 minute on a high flame till the chicken turns white.
4. Add strained yoghurt to this and mix it well.
5. Then, add salt, pepper and green chillies to it.
6. Close the lid and let it cook on a low medium flame for one whistle.
7. Let the pressure depressurize on its own.
8. Now, add the fresh cream into the mixture along with crushed dried fenugreek leaves and coriander leaves, and give it a gentle mix.
9. Garnish with butter and serve hot.

Rice & Breads

MISSI ROTI

A lightly-spiced, Punjabi speciality made with wholewheat flour and chickpea flour

Preparation Time : 10 minutes
Cooking Time : 15 minutes
Total Time : 25 minutes
Servings : 3-4

Ingredients:

Whole Coriander Seeds - 2-3 tsp
Carom Seeds - 2-3 tsp
Dried Fenugreek Leaves - 1 Tbsp

For The Dough:

Gram Flour (Besan) - 2 Cups
Whole Wheat Flour – 2/3rd Cup
Salt – 1 tsp
Turmeric – ½ tsp
Red Chilli Powder – 1 tsp
Dry Mango Powder – ½ tsp
Onion - 1 (finely chopped)
Pomegranate Seeds – 2 tsp (crushed)
Coriander Leaves – ¼ Cup (finely chopped)
Green Chillies - 3-4 (finely chopped)
Clarified Butter (Ghee) - 1 tsp
Warm Water - to knead the dough

Instructions

To Prepare The Coriander Masala Mix:

1. Dry roast the whole coriander seeds in a hot pan till they're fragrant.
2. Add carom seeds and put off the flame. Now, add the dried fenugreek leaves.
3. Grind the mixture into a coarse powder. Keep it aside.
4. Transfer all the rest of the ingredients except ghee and water to a wide bowl along with the coriander powder mix.

5. Mix and gradually add warm water to form a smooth dough.
6. Apply 1 tsp of clarified butter (ghee) and knead again. Now, cover the dough with a kitchen towel.
7. Let the dough rest for half an hour.
8. Once the dough has rested, knead it again and roll it into medium-sized balls.

To Prepare The Roti:
1. Roll one of the balls into a circle of 5-6 inch.
2. Apply a few drops of salt water (mix 1 cup of water with ¼ tsp. of salt) on one side of the roti with fingers.
3. Paste the watery side on a hot griddle. Gently press it with a napkin.
4. Turn the griddle upside down and cook the roti on the direct flame until brown spots begin to appear.
5. Keep moving the roti to roast it from all the sides.
6. Turn the griddle and cook the roti for another minute.
7. Now, apply some clarified butter (ghee) on top of it and remove it from the griddle.
8. Serve hot.

ALOO MASALA POORI

A popular Indian, staple breakfast, lunch or brunch choice

Preparation Time : 15 minutes
Cooking Time : 15 minutes
Total Time : 30 minutes
Servings : 15 pooris

Ingredients:

Whole Wheat Flour - 1 Cup
Semolina – ¼ Cup
Salt – ½ tsp
Ginger – 1 (grated)
Asafoetida – ¼ tsp
Cumin Seeds – ¼ tsp
Red Chilli Powder – ½ tsp
Turmeric Powder – ¼ tsp
Fennel Seeds – ¼ tsp
Carom Seeds – ¼ tsp
Red Chilli Flakes – ¼ tsp
Clarified Butter (Ghee) - 2 Tbsp
Green Chillies - 3 (finely chopped)
Coriander Leaves - 1 Tbsp
Boiled Potatoes - 2 (grated)
Oil - ½ tsp
Oil - for frying

Instructions:

1. In a wide bowl, mix all the ingredients, together (except oil).
2. Knead it to form a slightly-firm dough (if required, add 1 Tbsp. of water).
3. Apply 1/4 tsp oil over the dough and cover it with a kitchen towel. Allow it to rest for a minimum of 20 minutes.
4. Once the dough has rested, shape the poori dough into round, medium-sized or slightly smaller balls.

5. Apply oil to all the dough balls. Do not dust any flour on them or you will find dark burnt flour particles in the oil.
6. Roll the dough evenly into circles which are neither too thin nor too thick.
7. Heat oil for deep frying in a wok. Add one poori at a time.
8. Fry till the poori is golden brown and crispy from all the sides.
9. Drain the poori on an absorbent paper to remove the excess oil.
10. Serve hot.

Note: Make sure that the oil is neither too hot nor cold. If it's too hot, then the poori will get brown (rather, burnt) way too quickly within seconds and if the oil is not hot enough, then the poori will absorb all the oil from the dough and remain un-cooked.

GARLIC NAAN

A classic yet delicious, traditional Indian flat-bread

Preparation Time : 2 hours 15 minutes
Cooking Time : 20 minutes
Total Time : 2 hours 35 minutes
Servings : 6-7

Ingredients:

All-purpose Flour (Maida) - 2 ½ Cup
Yoghurt – ¼ Cup
Sugar - 1 tsp
Salt – to taste
Baking Powder - 1 tsp
Baking Soda - a pinch
Oil - 2 Tbsp
Water - to knead the dough.
Onion seeds (Kalonji) - 1 tsp

For Garlic Naan:

Butter - 3 Tbsp (melted)
Garlic – 3 (crushed & finely chopped)
Coriander Leaves - 2 Tbsp
(Mix together Crushed garlic and chopped coriander leaves to the melted butter]

Instructions:

1. In a bowl mix together yoghurt, sugar, baking powder and baking soda till the sugar dissolves.
2. Now in a separate bowl mix together salt and Maida. Make a well in the centre and add 2 Tbsp of oil. Note that, you can even add butter instead of oil.
3. Knead the mixture into a soft and pliable dough by gradually adding water for about 5 minutes.
4. Cover with the damp cloth and let the dough rest for minimum 2 hrs.
5. After the dough has rested enough, gently punch down the dough.
6. Make medium sized balls from the dough.
7. Flatten slightly and sprinkle some flour on the dough as well as on the rolling board.
8. Sprinkle some onion seeds (Kalonji) on the rolled dough
9. Roll to 6-7 inches elongated circle.
10. Heat a skillet over medium-high heat.
11. Transfer the rolled naan onto the hot skillet
12. Let it cook for a couple of minutes until you see the bubbles on the top.
13. Brush the naan at this point with the prepared garlic butter (Optional).
14. With the help of a tong, remove the naan from the skillet, flip it over and transfer the naan directly to the flame.
15. Cook the naan for 15-20 seconds directly on the flame until, it's nicely golden brown from both the sides.
16. Take off from the flame and brush more garlic butter on top of the naan, as per your preference.
17. Serve Hot.

BEETROOT POORI

A colourful, Indian fried bread full of nutritious value

Preparation Time : 45 minutes
Cooking Time : 20 minutes
Total Time : 1 hour 5 minutes
Servings : 4-5

Ingredients:

Whole Wheat Flour – ½ Cup
Fresh Beetroot – ¾ Cup (made of 1 medium beetroot)
Semolina – 1 ½ Tbsp
Carrom Seeds – ¼ tsp
Salt - to taste
Oil - for deep frying

Instructions:

1. To make the beetroot juice : Pressure cook the beetroot in enough water for 2 whistles.
2. Let the pressure depressurize on its own. Drain and let it cool completely
3. Now peel and roughly chop it and grind it with 2 Tbsp of water to make a smooth paste.
4. Extract the juice through a sieve and set it aside.
5. In a wide bowl, mix all the dry ingredients including the whole wheat flour, carom seeds, semolina and salt.
6. Knead it, to form a slightly-firm dough by gradually adding the beetroot juice (if required, add a little water).
7. Apply ½ tsp of oil and cover. Let it rest for 10 minutes.
8. Once the poori dough has rested, shape them into round, medium-sized or slightly smaller balls.
9. Apply a little oil to each dough ball. Do not dust any flour or else, you will find dark, burnt flour particles in the oil itself.
10. Roll the balls of dough evenly into circles which are neither too thin nor too thick.

11. Heat the oil for deep frying in a wok.

12. Add one poori at a time. Fry till the poori turns golden brown from both the sides.

13. Drain the poori on an absorbent paper to remove the excess oil.

14. Serve piping hot.

Note: Make sure that the oil is neither too hot nor cold. If it's too hot, then the poori will get brown (rather, burnt) way too quickly within seconds and if the oil is not hot enough, then the poori will absorb all the oil from the dough.

SPINACH POORI

A delicious & vibrant, fried Indian bread which makes a wonderful breakfast idea

Preparation Time : 10 minutes
Cooking Time : 15 minutes
Total Time : 25 minutes
Servings : 18-20 pooris

Ingredients:

Whole Wheat Flour - 2 Cups
Fresh Spinach Leaves - 3 Cups (Cleaned & washed)
Boiling Water - 3 Cups
Ginger - 1 inch
Green Chillies - 2
Carrom Seeds – ½ tsp
Asafoetida - a pinch
Water - ¼ - ⅓ Cup
Salt - to taste
Oil - for deep frying

Instructions:

1. To make the spinach puree : Blanch the spinach leaves in boiling water.
2. Strain and grind them into a fine paste along with ginger and green chillies. Keep it aside.
3. In a wide bowl, mix all the dry ingredients like whole wheat flour, carom seeds, asafoetida, and salt together.
4. Knead to form a slightly-firm dough by gradually adding spinach puree (if required, add a little water).
5. Apply ½ tsp. of oil and cover. Let the dough rest for 10 minutes.
6. Once the dough has rested, shape the poori dough into round, medium-sized or slightly smaller balls.
7. Apply a little oil to each dough ball. Do not dust any flour or else, you will find dark, burnt flour particles in the oil itself.
8. Roll the balls of dough evenly into circles which are neither too thin nor too thick.

9. Heat the oil in a deep frying pan.
10. Add one poori at a time. Fry till the poori is golden brown from both the sides.
11. Drain the poori on an absorbent paper to remove the excess oil.
12. Serve hot.

Note: Make sure that the oil is neither too hot nor cold. If it's too hot, then the poori will get brown (rather, burnt) way too quickly within seconds and if the oil is not hot enough, then the poori will absorb all the oil from the dough.

VEGETABLE BIRYANI

An Indian rice dish with vegetables cooked under a 'dum' technique

Preparation Time : 20 minutes
Cooking Time : 50 minutes
Total Time : 1 hour 10 minutes
Servings : 3-4

Ingredients:

For The Vegetable Marination:

French beans - ½ C chopped

Green Peas - ½ C

Cauliflower florets - 1 small

Carrot cubed - 2 small

Clarified Butter (Ghee) - 1 Tbsp

Saffron - a pinch

Cumin seeds - ¼ tsp

Ginger - Garlic paste - 2 Tbsp

Salt - to taste

Red chilli powder - ½ tsp

Turmeric powder - ½ tsp

Coriander powder - ½ tsp

Mace powder (Javitri) powder - ¼ tsp

Green cardamon powder - ¼ tsp

Mint leaves - 4-5

Strained yogurt - 1 Cup

*Brown fried onions - ¼ cup

Oil - 1 Tbsp

Onion - 1 medium size sliced

Mace (Javitri) - 1 whole

Cumin seeds - ½ tsp

Water - ¼ cup

Cloves - 2

For The Rice:
Basmati rice - 2 Cups (washed & soaked for 30-40 minute)
Black peppercorns - 4
Whole spice - 4 (optional)
Cloves - 2
Black cardamom - 1 big
Mace (Javitri) - 1 whole
Bay leaf - 2

Saffron & Milk Mix:
Oil - 1 Tbsp
Salt - ¼ tsp
Warm Milk - 1 Cup
Saffron - A pinch
Green chillies - 2 slit lengthwise
Clarified butter (Ghee) - 1 Tbsp
Kewra water - 1 Tbsp
Rose water - ½ Tbsp
Water - ½ cup

For Garnishing:
Mint leaves - few
Brown fried onions - ¼ Cup
All-purpose flour (All-purpose flour) - to make a dough to seal the vessel

* For The Brown Fried Onions:
1. Deep fry the sliced onions till it evenly turns golden brown in colour.

2. Strain them and place them on an absorbent paper and spread them loosely.
3. They are ready to use.

Instructions

1. Mix together all the ingredients for the vegetable marination french beans, green peas, cauliflower florets, carrots, clarified butter, saffron, cumin seeds, salt, red chilli powder, turmeric, ginger garlic paste, coriander powder, mace powder, green cardamom powder, mint leaves, yogurt, fried onions and keep it aside.
2. Heat 1 Tbsp of oil in a heavy bottom pan.
3. Add mace, cloves and cumin seeds and let it splutter.
4. Add the marinated vegetables. Sauté for few minutes
5. Add ¼th C of water
6. Cook for about 10 minutes or sauté till ¾ cooked.

To prepare the Rice:

1. Boil the water with 2 tsp of salt
2. Add all the whole spices black peppercorns, mace, cloves, big cardamom and bay leaves.
3. Add rice to the boiling water and cover and cook on a low flame, till done.
4. Strain and keep it aside.

For the saffron infused milk:

1. Heat the ghee in a pan add green chillies and saffron and sauté for few seconds.

2. Now add milk, ½ cup water, rose water and Kewra water and salt. Give it a stir. Take off from the flame and keep it aside.

For Assembling the Biryani:

1. Layer ½ quantity of rice over the ¾th cooked vegetables and spread it evenly throughout.
2. Pour ½ quantity of the saffron infused milk on the top of the rice.
3. Garnish with few brown onions and mint leaves.
4. Arrange the remaining vegetables followed by remaining rice.
5. Pour the remaining milk mixture and garnish with the few mint leaves and fried onions.
6. Place a kitchen cloth on the top of the rice. Now cover the handi with the lid. Apply dough all around it to seal the vessel.
7. Cook it on dum (slow flame) for 20 mins. Take off from the flame.
8. Let it sit for 10 minutes before you open the lid.
9. Your dum biryani is ready.

Note:

- Scoop out biryani from the edges of the pan, making sure not to break the rice grains.
- Vegetable biryani has to be made with long grain rice like basmati rice. Do not try and replace basmati rice with other normal rice.
- The quantity of the spice can be increased as per your taste.
- If you don't have heavy bottom pan to dum the biryani then you can keep a griddle under the cooking pan for cooking.

CHANNA PULAO

An Indian pulao recipe which is usually served for lunch or dinner along with raita

> **Preparation Time : 15 minutes**
> **Cooking Time : 15 minutes**
> **Total Time : 30 minutes**
> **Servings : 3-4**

Ingredients:

White Chickpeas (Kabuli Channa) - 1 Cup (washed & soaked overnight)

Basmati Rice - 1 Cup (washed & soaked for 20 minutes and strained)

Oil - 3 tsp

Onion - 1 (finely chopped)

Ginger-Garlic Paste - 1 tsp

Tomato - 1 (finely chopped)

For Whole Spice Mix:

Bay Leaf - 1

Star Anise - 1

Cloves - 5

Cumin Seeds - 1 tsp

Cinnamon Stick - 1 inch

For Dry Spice Mix:

Mango Powder – ¾ tsp

Garam Masala – ½ tsp

Turmeric Powder – ¼ tsp

Kashmiri Red Chilli Powder – 1 tsp

Coriander Powder – ½ tsp

Cumin Powder – ¼ tsp

Dried Fenugreek Leaves – 1 tsp

Salt - 1 tsp

Water - 2 Cups

Coriander Leaves – a handful (for garnishing)

Instructions:

1. Pressure cook the soaked chickpeas in 3 cups of water along with ½ tsp salt for 10 minutes on a medium flame.
2. Let the pressure depressurizes on its own. Drain the water and keep it aside.
3. Heat 3 tsp oil in a wide pan and add whole spices like bay leaf, star anise, cloves, cinnamon stick, and cumin seeds to it. Sauté for a few seconds, till it's fragrant.
4. Add chopped onions to it and sauté till the onions turn translucent.
5. Then, add the ginger-garlic paste and sauté, till the raw smell disappears.
6. Now, add the tomatoes and salt.
7. Cook till they turn soft and mushy.
8. Finally, add all the dry spices like turmeric powder, chilli powder, coriander powder, cumin powder, garam masala, mango powder, dried fenugreek leaves. Mix everything well.
9. Add in the drained, boiled chickpeas and sauté the entire mixture for about 7-10 minutes on a medium-high flame till the chickpeas are well-coated with the masala.
10. Add the strained rice to it and gently toss the mixture.
11. Then, add 2 cups of water and pressure cook for 1 whistle.
12. Let the pressure depressurize on its own before opening the lid.
13. Once cooked, give it a gentle mix. Garnish it with coriander leaves and serve.

TAVA PULAO

The most popular, quick & easy-to-make recipe for Mumbai-style street food

Preparation Time : 10 minutes
Cooking Time : 20 minutes
Total Time : 30 minutes
Servings : 3-4

Ingredients:

Cooked Rice - 2 cups
Butter - 2 Tbsp
Cumin seeds - 1 tsp
Onion - 1 medium (sliced)
Carrot - 1/4 Cup (slided)
Cabbage - 1 cup shredded
Capsicum -1 medium sliced
Peas - 1/4 cup boiled
Ginger garlic paste - 1 Tbsp
*Red chilli paste - 1 Tbsp
Salt - to taste
Lemon juice - 1 Tbsp
Pavbhaji Masala - 1 Tbsp
Coriander leaves -for garnishing

*For The Red Chilli Paste

Whole Kashmiri red chillies - 6-7 soaked overnight

Cumin seeds - 1 tsp

Garlic - 5 cloves

(Blend it together to make a smooth paste)

Instructions:

1. Melt 2 Tbsp of butter in a wide frying pan or griddle.
2. Add cumin seeds and let it splutter.
3. Add onions and sauté for a minute till translucent (do not brown).
4. Add ginger garlic paste and sauté, till raw aroma disappears.
5. Add shredded cabbage. Mix well and let is cook for 3-4 minutes.
6. Add Capsicum, boiled peas and chopped tomatoes. Mix well.
7. Add coriander leaves, red chilli paste, pav bhaji masala, coriander powder and salt. Stir and sauté for about 6-7 minutes till the oil oozes out. .
8. Add 1 Tbsp of lemon juice.
9. Add cooked rice and toss it gently and uniformly.
10. Garnish with coriander leaves.
11. Serve hot with papad and raita.

CHICKEN DUM BIRYANI

A traditional Hyderabadi biryani and an aromatic delicacy loved by all

> **Preparation Time : 20 minutes**
> **Cooking Time : 1 hour 55 minutes**
> **Total Time : 2 hours 15 minutes**
> **Servings : 4-5**

Ingredients:

Chicken - 500 g

For The Chicken Marination:

Cumin Seeds – ¼ tsp.
Red Chilli Powder - 1 tsp.
Kashmiri Red Chilli Powder – 1 tsp.
Salt - 2 tsp.
Turmeric Powder – ½ tsp.
Oil – ⅓ Cup
Lemon juice – 1 Tbsp.
*Brown Fried Onions - 2 medium size
Strained Yoghurt - ⅓ Cup
Ginger-Garlic Paste – 1 ½ tsp.

For The Mint & Coriander Paste:

Mint Leaves - 1 ½ Cup
Coriander Leaves - ¾ Cup

Green Chillies - 2
Ginger - 1 inch
Garlic - 5 cloves
Water – 1/8 Cup
[Blend it all, together, to form a thick paste]

For The Rice:
Basmati Rice - 400 g (2 Cups) (washed & soaked for 30 minutes)
Black Peppercorns - 4
Whole Spice - 4 (optional)
Cloves - 4
Green Cardamom - 4
Cinnamon Sticks - 2
Bay Leaf - 1
Water – 4 Cups
Warm Milk - 1/4 Cup
Saffron - a pinch
Clarified Butter (Ghee) - 2 Tbsp
Biryani Masala - 2 tsp
Kewra - 1 Tbsp
Rose water - 1 Tsp
Mint leaves - For garnishing
All-purpose Flour (Maida) – for the dough to seal the vessel
*Rice water - 1/2 Cup (the starchy water left over after rice is cooked)

Instructions

*For The Brown Fried Onions:

1. Heat the oil for deep frying in a pan.
2. Add the sliced onions and fry till they turn golden brown.
3. Strain them and place them on an absorbent paper. Spread them loosely.
4. They are now ready to use.

For The Chicken Marination:

1. Take a heavy bottom pan and add all the chicken pieces to it along with 2-3 tsp. of mint and coriander paste.
2. Now, add all the ingredients for the marination including cumin seeds, red chilli powder, Kashmiri red chilli powder, salt, turmeric powder, oil, lemon juice, strained yoghurt, and ginger-garlic paste and ½ quantity of fried onions to it.
3. Mix it well so that the entire chicken is well-coated with the marination.
4. Refrigerate it for a minimum of 1 hour.

For The Rice:

1. Boil 4 Cups of water in a pan with 2 Tbsp of salt (the water should taste very salty).
2. Add all the whole spices like black peppercorns, cloves, green cardamom, cinnamon sticks and bay leaf to this water.
3. Now, add the strained rice and cook till $3/4^{th}$ done. Strain the cooked rice. (preserve half cup of *rice water for the later use.)
4. Remove the whole spices. (optional)

For The Saffron-infused Milk:

Add a pinch of saffron to $1/4$ cup of warm milk and mix. Keep it aside.

For The Biryani Masala:

Heat 2 Tbsp of clarified butter (ghee) in a pan, add the biryani masala to it and mix. Take off from the flame.

For Assembling The Biryani Masala Mix:

1. Layer the marinated chicken in a heavy bottom pan. Spread the cooked and strained rice over it evenly throughout.
2. On top of this mixture, spread some saffron-infused milk, kewra water, rose water, $1/2$ cup of rice water and the biryani masala mixture.
3. Garnish it with fried brown onions and mint leaves
4. Place a kitchen cloth on top of the rice. Now, cover the handi with the lid. Apply a layer of dough all around it to seal the vessel.
5. Cook it for 30 minutes on lowest flame and then, keep the griddle under the vessel and dum (or slow-cook) it for another 25-30 minutes.
6. Let it set for 10-15 minutes more before you open the lid.
7. Your chicken dum biryani is finally ready to serve.

Note:

- Scoop out all the biryani from the edges of the pan, all the while ensuring that you do not break the rice grains.
- A chicken dum biryani has to be made with long grain rice like basmati rice. Do not try and replace basmati rice with other normal-sized rice.
- The spice quantity of this form of biryani can be increased as per your taste.

www.ingramcontent.com/pod-product-compliance
Lightning Source LLC
LaVergne TN
LVHW081451060526
838201LV00050BA/1763